POSITION & RELATION

Other books by India Radfar

India Poem
Pir Press, 2002

the desire to meet with the beautiful
Tender Buttons Books, 2003

Breathe
Shivastan Publications, 2004

12 Poems That Were Never Written
Seeing Eye Books, 2006

POSITION & RELATION

India
Hixon
Radfar

Barrytown/Station Hill

I have been stealing, stealing images, but I don't care. I want the images that I have taken. I have always loved dreams. I want the words that are really dreams.

Published by Barrytown / Station Hill Press, Inc. in Barrytown, New York 12507, as a project of the Institute for Publishing Arts, Inc., in Barrytown, New York, a not-for-profit, tax-exempt organization [501(c)(3)], supported in part by grants from the New York State Council on the Arts.

E-mail: publishers@stationhill.org
Online catalogue: http://www.stationhill.org

Thanks to Edward Sanders for permission to use his Glyphic Translation of Sappho Quatrain. Thanks to Mindmade Books (formerly Seeing Eye Books) for permission to reprint "12 Poems That Were Never Written," © 2006. The poem on p. 9 first appeared in The Chronogram, December 2004. The poem on p. 41 first appeared in Xantippe, Vol. 4-5, 2006-2007.

Cover art by Saskia Friedrich
Cover and interior design by Susan Quasha

Special thanks to the late Saul Bennett, to Bernadette Mayer & Melanie Shih for their knowledge (poetic & medical), even though their advice was at odds, to Bernard, Aram, and all of my family, and extra special thanks to Leila for being born.

Library of Congress Cataloging-in-Publication Data
Radfar, India.
  Position & relation / India Radfar.
    p. cm.
ISBN 978-1-58177-110-7 (alk. paper)
I. Title. II. Title: Position and relation.

PS3618.A349P67 2008
811'.6—dc22

                              2008028764
Printed in the United States of America

a formal farewell to the rivers and mountains

CONTENTS

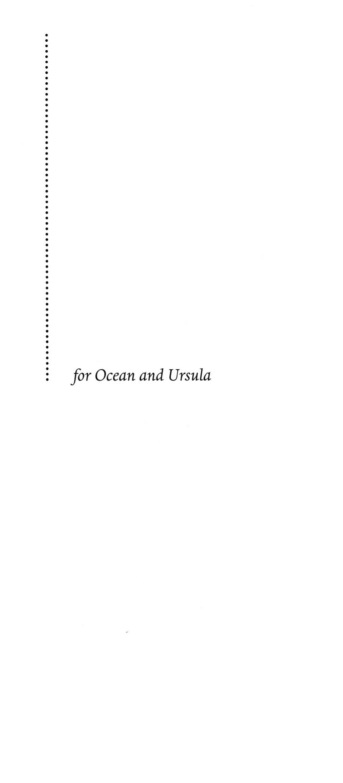

for Ocean and Ursula

12 POEMS THAT WERE NEVER WRITTEN

These poems
have no subject
  you must take them
as they are

    If,

    suddenly

the bare tree
  threatens to retell
  the endless story
of the plum blossom,

  leave it –

When the poems end
  the plum's story
    will begin again

there is nothing you can do

    you will definitely

eat it

    but now,
    for the sake of these

poems,

    don't be hungry.

This is a poem about loss

it comes to me in the morning
when I open my eyes

This is a poem
I can't admit to writing

when I tell my husband
about it
he smiles at me
out of surprise

You don't need
to write this poem

but the poem comes
and tells me differently
maybe I should also
say,
you are not
for me

but verses can fall out
at any time

(   )

with as few words
  as possible
as raw as it feels
   to live

       ⊕

          ⊕

Once I saw a painted lizard
  white from lack of sun
  emerge on its one day of the year

      into this very room

   when I came back to contain her
  she was mysteriously gone

   the earth is terrible and
    it has taken her

    inside,
    there is the poem

At what loss do I receive it?

  with the poison of the earth
I fill myself
how repulsive it is
   where I must go.

This poem was passing
right by me but I
 decided not to stop it

 it turned around to
look at me

 we stared hard
at each other
in the dusk

 then the poem went
its direction and
 I went mine

 occasionally we turned
around to look at
 each other

a moment before it was
  completely gone, I had
 a sudden fear it would
  chase me.

This poem doesn't have

to worry

because it was
never mine
I could never write it
so,
anything it hopes
to be
it can be

with no interference
on my part

⊕

⊕

There is still one more
poem to go for tonight
I hold it in my palm
it weighs nothing
and of course
it can't be seen
it's warm
I fold my fingers around it
and squeeze
it laughs
it says go to sleep

does it really say that?

⊕

I close my eyes
  and look,
I find this poem

⊕

For Heather Hutchison

Traverse my lines and you
  will find me
    I am

      the unseemly creation
    behind this artifice of beauty

you will want to reject me
  don't
I am in need of you

exhale me,
  but live with me
because strangely

    I am also the light

I fill involuntarily the empty land and
  overflow the boundaries
    you have set me

First I went to the basement
rather unhappy there
I brought friends
and we
talked and laughed and

filled the strange room

with light

Then I slipped to
the basement of the basement
they looked in on me
one by one
through a crack in the floor

my husband brought me food
and kept me company
but no one knew how to

free me

Then I dropped to
the basement of the basement

of the basement

here, unfortunately
no one could find me.

For Cecília Vicuña

This poem is another's
  all evening around my head
    I saw it
    I listened to it
    I really believed in it

  but it's not mine
why is that so hard
  to understand?

I cannot write it
    for myself
    for you
      for any one

This poem is letting go
of everything it carries

it is emptying its
    hands
  of everything

    it is

    carrying nothing
it moves and turns

NATURAL MEGARON*

---

* A natural megaron is the site of a temple, chosen for its view and position within the landscape.

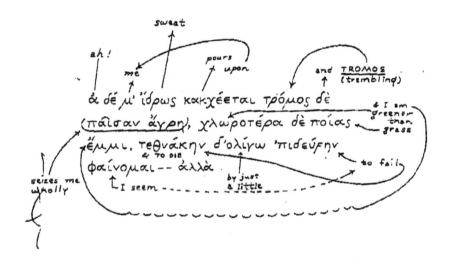

Glyphic translation of Sappho quatrain by Edward Sanders

In honor of the 7th Century B.C. Greek poet, Sappho.

The hill that inspired these poems is the one near her birthplace, the ancient town of Eressos on the island of Lesbos; a hill climbed by her, as local legend tells us, to write …

These poems were written at the Mediterranean outlook of California Quarry in Woodstock, NY.

Preface

Climbing under the hot sun made me reel. In my dis-
orientation, I unearthed the broken pieces, waves of
clay standing out in relief on the ground. The heat then
released a second relic, ancient as longing, into the air.
It felt like power. The emotion was not mine but acted
upon me. I wondered how much of its strong current
had to stay and how much I could let go forever. Clutch-
ing the earthly remnants, I stepped out of the spiral that
had formed around me. Like a cloud it dissolved in all
the places where before it had bound me. I call that spiral
ambition.

All Fall

wind means crazy in some languages
removes all thought
cries from the future
soaked with rain.

the moon set
the sun rose, then all day
passed before the baby came
and by the time the sun set
orange, the baby, dead
was in her arms
the union of birth and death
sky changes, it cannot stay the same
metamorphic, no explanation
sliding like a cloud between

almost forgot where this was
almost felt like down below for a moment

goodbye, up high
don't worry, big stone tender
it is dark now, and raining

here, orange truck of the sky
comes an order for the living
live in the dark, in the disappearances
go in
sleep and dream
use the wind
as a bed

Better

visualization of climbing a mountain:

rain falling
animals circumambulating
to exhale the air of Eressos
here I am
cloth of shadow
waiting for my body
to come into the foreground

rain falling
the mist appears
in what curve
of what thought
of what mountain

Grammar

Of course there would be heat
from this hill of pines
and their sad smell
high above the human valley
so full of ingratitude

the humility of this hilltop
its crescent proportions
reclining against the sea
under hot filaments of light

what are details, what is description?
this is how she got away

the endless flight of yellow butterflies
the tumescent rock pile
an appearance of mountains
a secret moment in the kitchen
the poet's ambition in the dirt
drawn by the wind
in a sort of madness

broken amphoras
landscape of breasts
these are not my tall pines
gnarled, neglected, shading only crows
disgusted, sick with ages

woman of land,
climbing the hill that makes you real
cultivate longing
be above sadness
make each island a love object to the other
curse a hundred steps of air

I am

when you came and left
the muse of joy
came anyway
she told us to
fill your clothes with flowers
she told us to
call your
sand lilies body
Ocean
she appeared to us
in celestial forms
your golden body
was her friend
she loved you
well

Dented

when I look down on the small indentation
in the forest that I call my home,
I feel no particular attachment to it.
I cannot get enough shelter under those
little yellow trees

I have given myself a constraint
and now I follow it
the mist appears, disappears
lifts, lowers
so far above my head it feels good

the desk below abandoned
base and pure, low and high
conceived and unconceived
jostling, situated
could turn into air up here

how delicate the future is
how many mistakes rush towards it
how melancholy our attempts to embrace it
how dangerous our love for it

are the ones who walk away
the future of us all?

Up along

I am ringed with mountains
a stone, pink within
playing at separating
body and soul

ice replaces flowers, climbing the dizzy trees
inside the house, a red glow
we take our clothes off
oh, that kind of fire
the dead of night
I have to leave
why did you leave without extinguishing the fire?
I didn't know it was a real fire.

where rocks and water meet,
a pink cavern filled with waves
the pink of the cave comes from a live organism
which covers the rock where it is naturally
submerged by water
pink, not green
breathing and kicking underwater,
barely alive

having to forget desire
unless this mountain opens right now
a nut opening its shell into a star.

Say it a

the first time I climbed Sappho's hill
I felt her ambition
but then the body's discomforts

Imagine arriving here
beside this other body of water
to be a climber of hills

I have put a constraint on myself
wholly unlike rhyming
a climbing restraint

do all hills lead to the same place
do all peaks join in the same circle of meaning

the brown beach makes the water come in dark green
instead of turquoise blue

to visualize
to feel ambition

the actual words of the text are not in this air
no exhaustion
no mad atmosphere here

to be a mountain
harvested for small words
today I feel different about your importance

It a

are you the ambition's author
or the author's ambition

purple glass
painted lizard
attempt to embrace
swirl of mist
desk below
birth of Ocean
so far above myself it feels good

are you ambition, muse
already above
coming out of my body

up is not a home
words can come
in no relation to down
could turn into air

delicate surrender
absorbing blue

mountain,
house I cannot leave

words of this dictation
in no particular order
blurring into fluency

Theater

I begin to step forward without being conscious of
sending myself forward
I pass the birch tree that spreads like an oak
the house where I think Judith lives and from where she
may have observed me
walking many times
ambition
the word appears written in air
I should write it on a rock in Tibetan or something.

The first time I climbed Sappho's hill, I felt her ambition
a strange thing to feel in the natural environment
I am making an experiment
to see if every mountain leads to the same place
except I don't have time for mountains
so I will be a climber of hills

Of the hills at either end of *Skala Eressou*, Sappho chose
the smaller one.

hills are patient with me
they let me stop for moments on them
without reaching any single point

now I am looking down on the landscape of this poem
but these hills are closed
no smells in the air
messy pattern of branches
ambition is half way up my body
Greece, you haven't given me what you promised yet

In winter, it's the birch that matter
the ice crashing down cannot be helped
it has a passion for falling

If I go to the second peak
I will increase my elevation
and from the second
join the third down a long path

why do I address the mountain
in the metaphors of home
can home give you a future
the way a mountain can?

Today was different
there were people and we were shouting to each other
from every peak

I or a

naked, vulnerable
hard to write
I don't know
passion seems alive
mountains give way
to mountains
kneeling in snow

too dark
inner heat
tree in front of me
gave the idea

Tap a

entering the imagination so intimately,
we then get expelled from it.
the play is gone, it is under the earth now
in the roots and the dark spaces.
the black lizard with white spots
lies undisturbed

In their house of earth
the play begins for them

dream fragment emerges, painfully,
the darkness is in it, self-evident
impossible to hold
impossible to let go of
we can't shame each other there
even if we touch each other

cold creature,
what do dreams speak of to you?
can passion live in the cold
or is that the realm of renunciation

author of ambition,
I cannot spring forth
I go to your center or
cling to your fingers
I wipe the ink off of the page
outside of a warm body
I am nothing, exactly nothing
but inside the swollen pile of rocks,
the fresh fruit of the mountainside

Lydian

having to forget desire
I cannot rush this
ink comes slowly
in the unreal moments and
wind makes its distinct approach
I was about to eat
but I woke instead
hungry
in the cold
scattering pages

Muse

the secret word behind ambition is muse
warm color lining my body, directing my hands
making me a statue of itself
remember the poet's ambition,
how much of it was confused by longings
wind was behind her ambition

Here I am, attaching feathers to the page
my presence on red paths
bringing flowers to the mountain
longing, when not satisfied, becomes ambition
the formula is simple
I found it sifting through dust

when she focuses her attention on you
clouds gather
and underneath them her town
and the rain the flowing waters
the writing of departures
I lift the umbrella
the pen passes through raindrops slowly
I get water on my fingers
speech patterns deteriorate
I realize I must be the one to introduce myself
hence the map on the reverse side of this page
a reference to an original page of this journal

I am half of many words
floating, raised up a little by a white haze on the water
of my shoreline

wind birds
birds of silence
the poet honored here
has flown away

PREPOSITION POEMS

I feel I must explain my process briefly:
I have used no prepositions.
Some languages, like Sanskrit, don't even
need them. And since these poems address
subjects where prepositions are far too
prevalent anyway, better that I simply
took them elsewhere.

Preposition ---

   a word
  (some languages)
expressing a relationship:

noun, pronoun or noun clause
        and
    another element
        such as
        verb
        noun
         or
        adjective

   e.g.

pine tree
the disappeared
forest
illuminating
distant
fragrance

I have come
invisible
the point
the air
the mists hide you and
float the velvet surfaces
your water
natural megaron
truly nowhere
my eye is your mountain
and everyone finds you
where I find you
please,
if you are something
tell me what
if you are not
tell me why

It tells place time quality
movement. It moves
what is it trying to express
why say it
look, find words, sounds
meanings
moving is good
there are other ways
        speaking

A little tiring
being coherent
trees had no leaves
heat was not oppressive
colors spoke differently
the scene appeared
somewhat lighter, higher
more self-reliant, perhaps
look, the words I have,
limited
is memory speaking?
I can't move
the words

I like circles
but circles need attaching
I lack something
which words are
when none come,
sentences end quickly
And time is present,
communicating itself
it fills me
flows
tremendous waves
breath
but
it's all slipping
fading
missing the page
take what you want
there is no employable device
everywhere I am
    becoming
  the same

hate eats you
my friend
undoes you
soon there will be nothing left
I spread my intimacies
the paper
not singular
paper
even spoken
or thought
you gather me
try
bring me
can you bring me back
once I've gone
and nothing is not
intimate?

gods and goddesses
hide the forest
sight takes them
and blindness takes them
I will miss
swimming the forest
bathing the cool river
forget little words and
reveal your fruit the sun
we can change the landscape
remove all position
the mind
and soon
the word
and later
the voice
but that is saying nothing
dream entered this place
wild mint
blue water
the jasmine and bee-filled air
imagine banishing all words
three letters and less
no I, no you

prepositions,
I love you
I love also
the language that isn't you
sticks scratch sand
black ink marks
brown leaf
a voice intones the night
the day the day
the night
  the temple drums
    say nothing
imagine
  singing the song
ceaselessly

we could replace
you
you
we could take you
and then bring you
it might be better
you
not there
I can change
you
you
and then change you
again
and you wouldn't know
the difference
because
the paper
you
you

Time
I will arrive
forsaking nothing
the broken air
what makes me sorry
my good heart
this prison

listen ---
dreams, ambient noise
music, just voices
just words
words used well
used plainly
even so
understanding comes hard
the river resplendent, resplendent
evening and morning
leave water's surface
water can't know
try, try knowing it
try telling how
water has a color
try entering it

try describing where you are
a heavy place
a cloud
it flows
try describing it
it feels good
the mountain comes
can you tell me more?
I like seeing the important things
that you can't see anywhere else
I would lower myself there
I would look hard
now you're getting it
my head like a swan's head
diving and returning
diving and returning

I go
water
enter its depths
travel
fathoms
arrival
see what is
what isn't

seen like this
opening the tree
whose leaves,
uncovered
come the sky
timeless shadow
consuming and forgetful
inhabit what then,
here, where
sensuality dissolves
limitless night, take me
dreams and
red lights fly

if the temple is removed
you still have the natural temple
you can stand
as they stood
contemplating the same
coming together
horizon
and what if
there never was a temple?
your words

        your eyes

air, mind and stone
stone, mind and air
piled everywhere

corner where
two bookshelves meet
half Indian half Greek
overhead light
interior and book-like
plum trees
blossom the cement
let me
build a temple
swell the corner
fill full
the red-cushioned
chair

Forget the Greeks
India manifested me
our mingling,
take a look
my heart is Greek
but I am fully
Indianized
a woman set free
really, all I want
is a moment's silence.

I know what comes next,
know the emotional space
the room I still have left
the moment cut, contained
I don't have enough words
entering your low doorway
ancient mind
first rejected birthplace
dream gods and sleep gods
my given language,
embedded, overbearing
sacrificing other clarities
slow   motion
    position
        relation

I sit hours
considering sculpted bodies
the chair small
red orange cushion
unbroken waves
wind, abundant wind,
I have been here
the voluptuous great pull
the body uncovered,
desire
there's no comfort
covering, uncovering
Position,
my ghost, my shadow
have I forgotten
everything?

these words that are
not allowed
who keeps them?
let their keeper
come and get them
I have reached
the edges
the outlying places
walking closer
doors open
lights spinning, bodies
shining, unattended

Position, I have sought
your proper place
have landed
snake-like
your tumescent
rock pile
grassy
wild
oracular
Position, I can't speak
all the places you are
my tendency
my perpetual circumstance
I will come, give me
entrance

kind movement
what have we done?
given speech another sound
marveling, incomplete
what is this
what kind place I step
and time, what sound here
encased
depends
needs so little
language fragments sense
time reduces fragments
rubbing the surface

whatever binds us
we are free

LUNG POEMS

I received the following poems gladly, the August 2003
3:15 a.m. writing (thank you, Bernadette Mayer). I
was visiting lake country and my father's grave and
I was also home. Sayner, Wisconsin and Woodstock,
New York. I was both places. The hour unfolded the
poems. It was an outpouring, mostly unremembered
when morning came. I wanted the night writing, but it
disturbed my sleep. I told my doctor. She was displeased.
Chinese medicine had taught her this displeasure. 3:15 is
lung hour, she said. And lung hour is grief's hour ...

((

to say you'll do something
and not do it
may be my tendency
I want to change
that
all night
remembering
what I said
    eyes close
  arm goes limp

I said

((

I don't know if
you want to
but you have to write
    drink boiled water
  tea,   get a little
money ready for
breakfast.   Not many
choices in India or
on a boat.

((

frozen
  mid-air

      It
clattered to the
floor
  So he has a
 father figure
what do you think, yes,

he loves it.

( )

how many times

   light off
I will it
to you

real
grace

   don't lift the
   pen from
the paper

))

sound of
ugliness
without sweetness.

quiet
the children
wanted

all over
quiet
settled in
no one

played.
what happens

in ten days
a plan

stand tall,
or die

has   time
who
has   time

no fruit

))

I've been
waiting

dreaming
dream
fitfully
started
wild animal

a privilege
to meet yourself

waking

so you'll
be calling, too?

full of
quiet breathing

my sister

had a
collection
of sparkle

she put her
books inside
dipped them.

))

let's see
  my child right here

so I   was roused
     early

still, dreams
  stir about
  unnatural

air moves
cool against me

I hesitate
  bear paws

  taking from the edges
    the center
      ungiving

  gave me time
   to separate
    my two selves
who wants two?

besides
all year

crop of memories
what are they for?
I only use them

in places like this

watch out
the longer I stay

here

the longer it takes
for the line to
fall in place

in this bed
    words swimming
we have to wait
        up
    nothing stirs

deep waters

important
        excited
        breathing
    independently   fills

        moving over

into the closed eyes

and yet
I want this
form of conversation

I rub my feet
  together
  my gesture of
    waking

((

why do this

I didn't know
what the alarm
was for

then, when I
remembered,
I thought I
was at Plum
Lake.   It was
easy

not because
we are in
the wilderness
we are
dedicated
to the
experiment
not because of that
eagle feathers
bad storyteller

it will never be
and yet
waiting
I sense
I'm not wanted
to do this

you must fly
when
he flies
speed away
on a horse

hug the
dark room tight

slow down
running

not alone
in the assignment

light on
reminds me
I have shame,
humility
so I don't speak
lost fathers
silence

time
runs on

with all
its numbers
of spirit

and
and
who knows

the trouble of this
solitary
activity
now with a
spectator
a reluctant one
asking
are you still writing

who's to say
that after I
drop the pen
and push this
away
I'm not

((

son and husband

    comfortable arms
      thick legs

    I have
almost   lost
the game

and then
    Danae
    you want to make
    her part of the story?

  soft rain

  calling out
    too fine

  chick pea
  flour

put some in
put everything in

    the
      rain
          comes
              down
however

with the
sound of wind
and no one
moves
I don't know
New York
the way you do

((

so,
lung   hour
  breathe extra
    hmm.

late. let me
  know fathers.
    Well, I can
    teach you

  she threw away
      all
    to the bottom

                    many, many
                      rings.
not able to realize
      the error.

      when I was sad,
      I dropped it.

((

who should remain
   in the circle?

those who wrote
   of bees
   or those who
   wrote of

   wild cats
    each category
named.   where
   do I fit in?

   Well, all right,
you can write about
whatever you want

   so many dried
    orange-purple
   pine needles
    that, for one,
I can tell you

   this time,
I think I am
  my son,
  who can't yet
write, and so
the categories

are futile
and everything
  drops away

I am buoyed

  up this time
by a leather
  book with
  soft white
  pages
we fall like
rain   like tears

()

draboom
    all of a sudden
    fire tower of dust

      too
    lugubrious

0

hero's heart

It changes
speech habits

you've been
someone else
somewhere else
the queen of Baghdad
is running out of time

okay
what else?

the queen's birth

that's another
story

spirited away

take us to

love land and
leave in the morning

here's   red   thrush

O

bright moonlit sky
stopped everything
I was doing
everything I was
thinking
opening sleep
of
light
that's not good enough
for you?
what are my options

another sky

please, that's dreary

my child clings to me

we have one flat pillow and
one puffy pillow
to sleep on.
bright   milkweed

sky   I put
my head on you
I get nearer and nearer

to you
bright ethereal
creature

spill on me
I need your wetness
all day long

◊

I will not leave
  the drawer empty
    tonight

the   reason   is
        obscure

maybe we were
an   anti-

    rainbow

  gushing light

people like us don't
sleep on these occasions

  yellow ebullience

my eyes sting
yellow trance

bewitches the sky
thank you
geometry of trees
thank you, crickets
thank you, yellow

light
            thank you

moon, for letting
me gaze upon you

tonight
above my bed
at the hour of
my waking
light streaming
out of you
magnificent

really
my house adores you

so do
I
moon   you equal

brilliance
look it up in the

dictionary
there can be no
mistaking you

you've
moved slightly

I move over
on the pillow
to where it's cool
there will be no
crying   admire
me admire me

I know
you'll be a wild
horse in the morning.

Photo of the author by Charise Isis